CLEVERMORE

Books by Steven Paul Winkelstein

THE SQUALL

ELEPHANT, ELEPHANT, COME ALIVE!

THE DIVING HORSE AND THE MAGIC WHISTLE

LUCY'S GREAT ADVENTURE

THE WILD MIND OF THE WINKLE

CAPTAIN KIDD AND THE JERSEY DEVIL (SUMMER 2015)

www.atruetaleofsurvival.com

STEVEN PAUL WINKELSTEIN

BRISKO

a true tale of Holocaust survival

ILLUSTRATIONS BY
DANA JULIANO

CLEVERMORE LLC
MYSTIC WATERS PUBLISHING
BOULDER   PHILADELPHIA   NEW YORK   MARGATE

Mystic Waters Publishing
Margate City, NJ 08402
in association with
Clevermore LLC
Boulder, CO 80304

This book is a non-fiction narrative based on
the real life stories of a Holocaust survivor. The author of this
book has obtained the rights and blessings to produce this material.

This book may be used freely in educational institutions everywhere, for
the purpose of education.

First Mystic Waters Publishing Edition 2014
Edited by Jody Berman

Common Core Standardized Review
assembled by educators
Douglas Winkelstein
Gretchen Van Duyne

Printed by CreateSpace, An Amazon.com Company
Available on Amazon.com and other book stores
Available on Kindle and other online stores

Manufactured in the United States of America

Library of Congress Control Number: 2014914371

ISBN-13: 978-0-9824498-6-8
ISBN-10: 0-9824498-6-0

TO THE CHILDREN
WHO DIED IN THE HOLOCAUST

NEVER AGAIN.

BRISKO

Contents

II. The Judenrat—23

III. A Dark Light in Tuchin—57

IV. Brisko—69

V. The Men Without Hearts and the Pheonix Rising—91

Appendix—i

I. Pogrom in Tuchin

Buried Alive

I woke up a few times before I could stay awake.

"Libe! Libe!" It was my father's voice.

"Here I am," I said.

I felt something hard under my head. I couldn't tell where I was.

"Libe!" My father shouted at me.

"I'm here!" I said.

The right side of my body felt a little numb. I tried to move my arm, but it would not budge. That frightened me. I went to sit up, but that didn't work either. I blinked.

"Libe!" My father continued to shout.

"Here I am!" I shouted. Then I realized that no sound came from my mouth. The shouting was in my head. I could make no sound, and my father could not hear me.

"Come, Isaak." It was my Uncle Fridal talking to my father. "She is gone."

No! I tried to say, but still no sound would come. *I'm not dead!*

They threw a sheet over my body and walked away. In my heart I felt more terror than I ever had.

They're going to bury me alive, I thought. I'm seven years old, and they're going to bury me alive.

I slept and woke several times. When I woke again, there was something heavy on my face. Soon I would be six feet under the ground, and there was nothing I could do about it, no matter how much I shouted. They would put me in the Tuchin graveyard. Only I would hear my final cries. The idea haunted me.

I knew what the heavy thing on my face was. It was a bible—it meant that I was dead. They had covered my face for the time being because they believed I was dead. Soon they would take me out of the house and put me in the ground.

I tried to scream again. Nothing. I wanted very much to weep. Only seven years old and buried alive. But I'm already getting ahead of myself. Let me tell you how it started.

Before the War

I was just a little girl when everything in my normal life began to change. Now I'm almost eighty, and I still remember. I remember my mother's smile. She was a petite woman with brown hair and hazel eyes. She had a quiet sweetness to her. I smile when I think about how she was before the war.

There are a lot of things I have forgotten. People do forget, you know; it's the nature of the mind. You'd be surprised what people can forget. But there are some things we can't forget, and not because these things are etched in stone in our minds. What I mean to say is, some things we're not *allowed* to forget. I remember because I have to. My story is not a pleasant one, and it doesn't come out like a fairy tale, where all the good guys stay alive and all the bad guys get what they deserve. It's a true story. It's my life. I'll tell you what I remember, not because I want to but because we're not allowed to forget.

I can remember my older sister, I'll tell you that. Channah was beautiful.

In 1939, just before World War II broke out, I was only five and she was eight. She didn't look much like me or my mother. Her hair was blonde and straight, and her eyes were blue. She didn't have any dark curls that were typical of so many little girls I grew up around. My hair was straight, too, but it was dark. Channah had my father's features. Channah and I did normal things that sisters do. We brushed each other's hair, played games.

On Shabbos, the Jewish Sabbath, we would walk through Tuchin, our little town. Back then it was part of Poland, but when World War II broke out Tuchin was brought into Ukraine and became part of Russia. That was only one of many changes that would come to pass.

I'd put on my little blue coat and lace up my brown leather boots, which had plenty of laces because they went up to my knees. I'd lace them all the way up, and my sister and I would go about the town. Tuchin wasn't the best place for Jews, even before the Russians came. Sure, it was a Jewish town, but our Ukrainian neighbors didn't like us very much. They threw stones, called us names. I remember they had a song for us whenever Christmas came around. "They killed him, they killed him!" they'd sing. You know, talking about Jesus.

There were a few well-off Jewish merchants in Tuchin, though most of us just got by. There were businesses from fabrics to wagons. The Jews worked hard. They were smart. We lived in my father Isaak's house, which was a nice house—newly built, roomy. It had a basement. My father and Uncle Fridal were good people, well respected in the community. Fridal had dark eyes. He was a dark-haired man, whereas my father was light, with blues eyes and blonde hair, which was where my sister got her looks.

On any given Saturday, sometimes with our father and mother, or sometimes alone, Channah and I would walk, laugh, and hold hands. We'd look at the shops on the street, pass the synagogues and the schools. It was a very tight community, very close. All of the Jewish families looked after each other. We all knew who everyone was. It was not a bad little town to be a child in before the Russians came, before my life changed forever.

Red Ribbons

It was night when the planes came. The engines screamed, waking the whole house. I threw off my bedsheets and in two steps covered the bedroom that I shared with my sister. I leapt into her bed. She held me.

"What is it?" I asked. "It's so loud!"

"Stop shaking," Channah told me. "It's only airplanes. Do you hear? Papa is coming now."

Our bedroom door swung open and hit the wall with a crash.

"Girls," he said, "get out of bed and put on your shoes and coats. Channah, there is no time to get dressed. Take your sister." My father looked worried. There was sweat on his brow and his words came out unsteady, disturbing the air.

"Where are we going?" I asked.

"Go with your sister," he told me, and then turned to Channah. "Your mother is waiting at the door. She will go with you."

I was afraid. It sounded like our father was not coming with us. I wanted to ask why. I wanted to hold onto him and never let go. But Channah grabbed my wrist and whisked me to the front door.

"Ow!" I said. "You're hurting me."

"Come on," she said, ignoring my protests.

True to my father's word, our mother was waiting by the door. She had on her coat and hurried us along. She stood on her tiptoes and briskly pecked my father on the cheek. Then we were gone. It all happened so quickly. *All* of this happened so quickly.

There were people on the street, and outside the noise of the planes was much louder. They roared through the sky like griffins. I could see that everyone was heading to the forest. I didn't understand what the sound of planes meant.

We ran and ran until we were out of the town and deep in the woods. My legs hurt. I remember when we were far away from the houses, my mother pulled us down underneath a great big tree. We sat, huddled there for hours. Although it was only the beginning of fall, my toes grew cold and numb.

"Mama," I whispered, after we'd been there for a while. "Take out my ribbons. The planes will see us."

My mother smiled. "No one can see your pretty red ribbons underneath this tree."

I nodded. I did not believe her, but I trusted her. And so I left the ribbons in, and we waited for the noise of those planes to die before returning to our home.

Change Comes to Tuchin

On September 1, 1939, the Nazi Party of Germany and their soldiers invaded Poland. This was the start of World War II. When the Nazis and Russians became allies, they split up Poland. The Russians took their portion and brought it into Ukraine. Our *shtetl* was caught in the middle of this horror. *Shtetl* is Yiddish for "small town." Yiddish is a sort of homemade language with bits of German, Hebrew, Aramaic, and Slavic. The word *Yiddish* means "Jewish."

It was the Russians who flew those planes we heard. Like some hard-to-believe parts of this book, it may seem like my red ribbons are made up just to tell a story, but I promise you they were real. In many ways they still are real. That memory of mine is of the night the Russians came, and it was on that night that, at the age of five, I was no longer a child. I ceased to live a normal life. Everything changed.

Because the Russians were Communist, we became Communist, which means that the state ruled every aspect of our lives. There was no more individuality. All of the Jewish shops were confiscated. They took my father's business, which sold grains. Whereas before we owned our belongings, our houses, our livelihoods, this was no more. The Russian government owned everything.

Shops weren't the only things the Russians took. Every night they came in with great big trucks. I remember watching from inside of the house, my father talking quietly in the corner of the parlor with my mother and my Uncle Fridal. Channah and I knew from watching out the window that the Russians weren't only taking our things—they were taking us.

The Jews they decided to take were sent away to Siberia. We didn't know it at the time, but ironically it would be these Jews who were actually being saved from what was to come. Have you ever heard the saying, "I'm going to send you off to Siberia if you're not behaving yourself"? That's where that comes from. Except in our case, it was not an empty threat. This was the reality. If you were a Jew who the Russians did not want around, you were sent away, sometimes never to see any of your family ever again. And so every night before the trucks came, we would go to see our grandparents and aunts and uncles in the other part of town and tell them good-bye, just in case. After that, Channah and I could only watch from the window and hope the Russians weren't coming for us.

This was the beginning of the end for most of the Jews in Tuchin. Before, there was help in the shops, help in the homes. Help was cheap in those days. Businesses were putting food onto people's tables and the community thrived. After the Russians came, our community began to die.

Under the Russian rule, life was hard. But still, in our little town we had no clue as to what was brewing in other parts of the world. We did not know what the Nazis were doing. We did not know that they were on their way. Compared with what was to come, we were living in paradise under the Russians.

Barbarossa

July 4, 1941. It was two years after the Russians came that the Nazis put into effect Operation Barbarossa. This was their plan to turn against their allies: the Russians. It was a turning point in the war. The Nazis came in to replace the Russians, which meant that for the next few years we had to experience the worst kind of people, those without hearts. This was the second sharp turn that our lives had taken in such a short time.

When the Nazis came, a lot of the Jews ran away with the Russians. We'd heard that the Nazis were bad, but we had no idea how bad they actually were. We didn't know about the concentration camps at that point. But a lot of people were afraid. We were used to living with the Russians by then, and no one liked the destruction that the Nazis brought with them. My father said we would stay. He said it was because of me and my sister.

"With two small children, we can't be running around," he told my mother, even as our neighbors were fleeing. I remember his sunken face, the worry, the weight of those great decisions on my father's shoulders.

With the arrival of the Nazis, a great alliance formed between them and the Ukrainians. This was mostly because of their mutual hatred for the Jews. Once all of the Russians had fled, we, the Jews, were the common enemy. Since the Ukrainians had hated us all along, they were very happy to help the Nazis with anything they needed. They gave the Nazis lists, long lists of Jews who the Ukrainians wanted beat up, robbed, or killed. These were Jews the Ukrainians had been waiting to get for years. They had grievances with these Jews for one reason or another. These grievances were nothing more than petty differences, nothing more than an argument over who was in line first at the market. The Jews had done nothing more than coexist with these people.

Evidently, my mother and father were not on those lists. But there were at least seventy Jews who were destined to die on that Friday night in July when the Nazis came. With the help of the Nazi soldiers, the Ukrainians began their pogrom, their *murder*, in our small village of Tuchin.

Here Come
the Nazis

I huddled by our window, staring into the dark street. Sarah, my mother's friend, was staying with us at the time. She had her baby with her. We were in the house that my father had recently finished building. It was a dream house. We had a large kitchen and a big room in the front, with beautiful stained-glass windows. It was me, my sister, my mother, and Sarah and her baby. My father had run into the woods with my Uncle Fridal and some of the other men. They didn't know what to expect. We all thought, here come the Nazis, marching into town, maybe they'll kill the men. So the men went and hid, and the women and children stayed at home.

As we huddled by the beautiful stained-glass windows, we had never been more uncertain of our future. Outside, we saw darkness and a few lamps lit. There was the sound of marching, hard boots on our paved roads. Channah held me.

"Papa will be alright," my mother told us. I think that maybe she was telling herself, too.

Sarah stood by us, cradling her baby. I wasn't sure what was going to happen. I was only seven years old at the time, but I knew that we were in more danger than we had ever been. Suddenly, my sister gasped.

"Look!" she said. "Down the road."

There was a group of Ukrainians turning down our street. I could see one German soldier with them, but the rest were just hoodlums. They moved loudly, shouting, talking, and laughing. They were having a good time. My sister's hand squeezed mine tightly. We grew nervous as they continued toward our house.

At this point we heard gunshots in the distance and people screaming. I don't think I was crying yet, not at that point, but I was worried because I saw that my mother was nervous. It took the German soldier and his Ukrainian lackeys about five minutes to work their way over to our house, and when they moved past our place my mother breathed a great sigh of relief.

"Wait a second!" the German soldier shouted. The whole gang paused.

We stood by the dark window barely breathing. The soldier had turned toward our house. He was staring at us. My mother's chest began to heave up and down.

"What is wrong with this house?" the German soldier asked one of the Ukrainians. He was asking about our home. It was a new house; it was a nice house. Why wasn't *it* on the list?

"Come on!" shouted one of the Ukrainians.

At once the men began to move toward us. My mother let out a deep moan and ran from the window. She went to the side of our home where the door was. She rubbed her hands against her dress, wiping off sweat. I remember my mother's friend sat on a chair, huddled over her baby, and rocked back and forth. And when they reached the door, the German soldier banged so hard that the baby woke and began to cry. That's when I started to cry, too.

"Open this door!" shouted the soldier.

My mother opened the door right away. I will never forget the terror in her eyes. Her jaw remained taught. She was frightened but ready to be strong for her children.

"Drag her out!" the soldier ordered, and then the Ukrainians attacked.

Right away they hit my petite mother on the head with their rifles, and then pulled her out of the house, onto the ground, and out into the courtyard. My sister screamed. They resumed beating my mother. I remember her small body against the road, the taller figures of the men looming over her, repeatedly striking without any humanity. She yelled for them to stop. I stood in the doorway screaming. At seven years old I saw those brutes kicking my mother. They hit her with rocks and bludgeoned her with the butts of their riffles. Blood gushed from her head, and I can still hear the sound it made. *Djjj! Djjj!* Like a drill.

One of the Ukrainians kicked my mother a final time. She had stopped screaming.

"It's finished," he said. "She's dead."

My face was wet with tears, and I was still screaming, but I couldn't hear anything except for the *Djjj! Djjj!* of my mother's bleeding head. I barely noticed my sister or my mother's friend and her crying baby. My sister grabbed me and pulled me down as the soldier and his men charged into the house. The back of some hooligan's hand met my face, and something heavy fell onto my head. Then I could not see and I could not hear. I fell from consciousness; a great blackness took over the entire world.

When I woke the first time, I had no idea what had happened to my mother. I had no idea about my sister, my mother's friend, or the baby. All I could think about was the bible over my head and the fact that they were going to bury me alive.

Several times I fell back into unconsciousness, and I was always surprised to wake up and discover that I was not dead or buried. The final time I woke during that living nightmare, I was on the couch, and I could hear my father and uncle working on my mother's wounds.

"Those devils beat your wife badly," said my Uncle Fridal. "Seven holes in her head. A broken nose. The bone over her eye snapped in two."

"She'll make it through," my father replied. His voice was low, sad.

My mother was alive! Then why did my father sound so downtrodden? And then I remembered—they thought I was dead. Only seven years old and about to be buried alive.

The Bible Lifted

In the morning I woke to the sound of my father crying, a sound I had rarely, if ever, heard before. I heard my sister speaking with my mother's friend, who was also crying.

"We'll bring her to the field," said Uncle Fridal. "Getzel Schwartzman informed me that's where they will bury the others."

My father didn't answer. He simply wept. I could imagine him nodding, or maybe just staring at my apparently lifeless body on the couch. Thank goodness my sister was brave and wanted to see my face one last time. It would not be the last time her courage would save my life. Thank goodness for her love. She walked over to me and bent down.

"Father," said my sister Channah. "I want to see her face one more time."

"Fridal," said my father. "Please."

My uncle lifted the bible from my face and I saw them. They were blurry and I could barely see past them, but as I looked from my father, whose cheeks were red and wet, to my uncle, and finally to my sister, their eyes widened and their breathing stopped. Despite the swelling, which had taken over my eyes, they saw my eyes move.

"She's—" my sister started.

"Alive!" exclaimed my father.

I cannot express how relieved I was. My death sentence was lifted. They kissed me, and touched me, and cried. I was unable to move. I wanted so badly to be picked up and hugged, but they were being tender with my body.

"Will she be like this forever?" Channah asked.

Channah had been spared a beating because of her blonde hair and her blue eyes.

"Fridal," said my father, ignoring my sister's question, "we have to get the children out of here."

My uncle nodded gravely, and I was told to go back to sleep. I remember I tried to sleep, but a terrible sound kept me up for hours to come. It was the sound of my father breaking the beautiful stained-glass windows of our front room and replacing them with ugly wooden boards.

The Man Who Brought Eggs

I woke up on a great big bed next to my mother and sister. My father had moved us to an apartment in the poor part of town. The apartment's owners must have been a family that my father knew. There were a few little children and their parents, but that's all I remember. It was a crowded place and the conditions were not what we were used to in the home my father had built.

My sister never left my side, as I was still paralyzed and couldn't speak.

"Please, take her," I remember my mother praying for me. "Make this terror stop for her."

My mother was bandaged up with the holes in her head and broken bones. I don't know how she managed. She, not able to stand her daughter being mute and unable to move, actually prayed for my death. She didn't want me to suffer.

Throughout the week after the pogrom, we were all nervous. We thought that at any moment the Nazi soldier, with his gang of Ukrainians, would come find us to finish off the job. My father and Uncle Fridal came and went, very mysteriously, with news that they shared only with each other and my mother. I could see right away that the Germans had brought a regime much more dangerous than anything the Russians had ever enforced. There were questions about keeping our house and ideas about running away. The whole world seemed to be changing again.

One day, when my father was feeling very down about the pain I was in, we were visited by an old customer of his, Pavlo. Pavlo was a poor farmer who lived a little ways west of the town, past the river. I never saw him because I was confined to the bed, unable to move around or talk. I always heard him, though. His voice was deep, loving. He would bring us food. What a wonderful man! And ... he was Ukrainian.

Why this man Pavlo cared so much for a business associate's family, I could not yet understand. But it was people like Pavlo that made surviving worth it in the end.

My father knew him through his grain business, and because Pavlo was poor, my father used to give him grain on credit. As we hid out in the poor family's apartment, Pavlo brought us eggs, milk, and butter. He came a few times, and every time he cried. That's how compassionate this man was.

At the end of the first week after the pogrom, we moved from the poor family's apartment to my grandmother's house, which was also in the poor section, though it was a large house. It had a big hall and a living room with a little black oven that had a chimney. My grandparents and my father's sisters lived there. Everyone would take turns tending the wood in the oven. The floor was nice, wooden. I remember my sister running around, playing and screaming, "I'm going to break your legs!" She made me laugh. We stayed in that house for a while. We had moved there because they'd killed my Uncle Fridal.

Our Fate

About a week after the pogrom, the Nazis gathered around twenty of the most influential and intelligent Jews in Tuchin and brought them to the town square. My Uncle Fridal, my mother's brother, was one of those Jews. There, the twenty Jews were hanged to death. Why? Because they were smart, because the Nazis felt threatened by them, because they had influence over the other Jews, but most essentially these twenty people were killed because the Nazis wanted to send a message: "If you are Jewish, this is your fate."

As I said, this is not a fairy tale; it is a true story. This is the story of how an unexpected friend saved me from the fate of my uncle and the 1.5 million children who were just like me who were murdered in the Holocaust.

II. The Judenrat

The Slaughterings

Over a year had passed since the Nazis raided our home, beat me and my mother, and killed my uncle. It was clear that the Germans were much worse than the Russians ever were.

Once my father felt things were safer, we moved back into the house he had built. It took a while, but I eventually regained the use of my legs and my speech. The swelling had gone down in my eyes, and my sight improved. I remember that my father would sit and massage my legs and my hand where a bone had broken. You know, it's actually a miracle that I'm alive today. Of course, some of the injuries never healed all the way through. My hand is still in pain to this day, and my brain was never quite normal afterward, though some would say that's just my personality coming through! What? You didn't expect that someone who has seen the horrors of the world could still maintain a sense of humor? What would be the point of surviving if I couldn't laugh anymore?

Anyway, it had been a long year, 1942. There were all kinds of changes in how we lived. It was a new period of adjustment. As my body was healing, the community I had grown up in was dying all around. Still we had no idea what the Nazis were doing around Europe. We didn't know about concentration camps yet or the mass killings. We had enough to worry about closer to home.

The moment the Nazis came to Tuchin, they set up what they called a Judenrat, or Jewish committee. The Judenrat was made up of Jews from the town. The task of its members was to do the Nazis' bidding. They were supposed to report where Jews lived and how many of them were there. They were ordered to take certain valuables from the other Jews in the community. For instance, a German officer might come to the head of the Judenrat with a list of goods. It would then be up to the Judenrat to find and confiscate those items. It was a disgusting charge, for the Jews to turn against their own people, and many of the Judenrat members would try their best to do as little harm as possible. But there were tough decisions that had to be made. In most cases, their families' lives were in danger.

It's important to keep in mind that the actions of the people involved in the Holocaust were not always as black and white as people might imagine.

Suppose you were told to take from a friend, a neighbor, a family member. You would refuse. I would hope you would refuse. But now, what if somebody asked you to do that or they would have your parents or your child killed or stolen away? How about if they told you to pick one of your parents to never see ever again? How could you choose? There is no morality in that choice. There is no good way to go. It's not a real choice. Do you see? When times become dark, as they had when I was a little girl in Tuchin, and our problems become heavier, the choices often become murkier. They are not really choices; they are sometimes death sentences.

The Nazis did not stay in the town with us. They would send in their Judenrat team of five or six, in big trucks, to collect and relay messages and orders. Getzel Schwartzman was their leader, and I learned that he had two sons who helped him with his various missions. They hated what they had to do, but nonetheless, in the beginning when all they were asked to do was ask for possessions, they reluctantly obeyed. So these men who made up the Nazis' Judenrat were often torn men. The hands of the Judenrat were used to strangle their own necks.

I can remember a man, probably Getzel, coming around to the houses. He asked for mink coats, diamonds, furs, leather goods ...

"And if you don't comply by next week on this day," he would say, "they're going to kill fifty people."

Because Tuchin was a *shtetl*, the people in the Judenrat knew who had what, and the Nazis knew that. But Getzel and his sons never liked what they were forced to do, and that would one day cause the German Gestapo, the Nazi secret police, a couple of headaches.

Sometimes when the Judenrat came to our house, my father would tell us to hide and be quiet. We would use the various hiding places that my father had built into the house. For instance, there was a place under the stairs in the front of our house. The staircase was made of only five or six stairs, but one of them was removable and beneath it was a hole for hiding.

The strange part about all of this was that even though we knew that lives were at stake, we still never wanted to part with our possessions. This was human nature coming out. Death was staring us in the face, and people would say, "Take the mink but leave the jewelry." Because of that attitude, a lot of people grew to dislike Getzel and his sons. There were arguments all the time, fighting and bickering, neighbor against neighbor. It was disgusting, and it was scary.

I was eight years old by then, and I was getting more aware of certain things going on around me. Aside from the arguing, there were whispers, secret meetings. The danger grew by the day. The Judenrat operated; the people obeyed. By the time I was walking again, about a year and a half had passed since the Nazis came with their pogrom. It was August 1942, and the Nazis had started building a ghetto in the poor part of town where my grandparents lived.

During this period we should have known that our time would come. Dangerous rumors floated about town. We couldn't face them. Nobody wanted to think that the end was near.

When the Nazis had first come into town, they'd made all of the Jews in Tuchin wear yellow stars so that everyone would know who we were, so that everyone would know who to hate, who to report on, who to abuse. As August moved into September and the ghetto was completed, all of us who wore those awful yellow stars with the black German word *Jude*, German for "Jewish," began to feel the pressure more and more. Still, we would not face our doom. We would not face this threat until it had us in its belly.

Early that September, I can remember my father and some men speaking together. I cannot remember exactly where, but I imagine it was in the kitchen of our home. I know that it would have been in the daytime because the Nazis had started a curfew at night, and the men would not dare to meet like this otherwise. My father's raised voice might have drawn me near their conversation. I can see myself creeping quietly down the hall and pressing my ear against the wall. The men spoke about terrible things. They usually spoke of these things only in secret, when they could.

I don't remember who the men were, but as I've said, I learned later of Getzel and his boys. And as they were the Judenrat, I can picture their frustration. I can imagine now how these men would have met in secret and spoke about such matters.

"This is Tuchin!" one would say, his voice low. "They need us. We are too productive to be in that kind of danger. What about the factory? Who would run it for them?"

"Don't you know that terrible things are happening all over Europe?" my father might have said. "It is not just here. There are terrible things afoot!"

We were beginning to learn that nearby towns were experiencing what the Nazis liked to call "liquidations," which were really just mass murders.

"No one would murder tens of thousands—"

"Hundreds of thousands!" my father might interrupt.

"Hundreds of thousands," the man with the deep voice, probably Getzel himself, would have answered. "They're just trying to frighten us."

"And you and your boys here?" My father's voice, I can imagine it trembling, shaking with a terrible mixture of fear and rage. I remember him arguing with men from the Judenrat, I really do. "What will you take from us next? Our daughters?"

My father maybe would have held his tongue then, and those men would have heard nothing except for the careful sound of their own chests rising and falling, unsteadied by their shared, unspoken fate.

Dolly

That September, in 1942, every Jew in Tuchin was ordered to move into the ghetto. The Nazis had chosen an interesting time to order the Jews into the ghetto; we were approaching Yom Kippur, one of the holiest of Jewish holidays. It is a time for the Jewish people to atone for their sins and start anew.

The Nazis were cruel, and their leaders were smart in war. They knew that the Jews would have their guard down during the time before a holiday. Think about how you and your family celebrate your favorite holidays, and realize that even for us, in time of war, we were with family and we were relaxed, with attacks and struggles being the farthest things from our minds.

The ghetto, as I mentioned, was constructed in the poorer part of town, where my grandparents lived. It wasn't as if the Nazis had torn down the old buildings to make a new one. The ghetto was basically an area of the town—thirty, forty, fifty houses maybe, where they fenced the Jews in like a quarantine, a people plagued.

My father, I remember, had dug a hole in our basement. He dug a big hole for the possessions we'd become attached to because he knew we were leaving, and I suppose somewhere, hidden in his wonderful mind, he thought that one day we might be coming back. Inside of the hole, he placed a huge pot, and inside of the pot he put all kinds of things: silver, gold, jewelry. I was allowed to put something in, too.

I remember walking downstairs into the basement, cold and dark. I held tightly to my most prized possession. It wasn't a jewel or an expensive coat. It was my dolly. I walked silently up to the hole where the pot was. I remember staring into the darkness and feeling frightened because I couldn't see the bottom. I didn't know how far it went or what I would find there if I fell into it. I held my dolly out over the hole and closed my eyes. Then I let go, and it seemed like forever before there was the soft sound of fabric hitting the pot. I remember that.

I still remember my little dolly, with her little dress and curly hair. I loved her so much. My father let me put her in that pot with all the silver and gold and whatever other possessions he thought were valuable. I remember when I dropped my dolly into that dark hole, I knew in my blood I'd never see her again.

The Principal

It was September 18 or thereabouts. Little did we know that our nightmare was just beginning. On that September day, as we packed up our home, our belongings, our life, we heard a knock at the door—the door on the house my father built. It was the house we were fleeing now, with our only anchors remaining in a dark hole in the basement. But even I knew then, those items were nothing more than the last feeble straws of our quickly disappearing wishful thinking. They would be no more of a lifeline to us than a buried bar of silver would be to a starving dog.

Let me tell you about our strange visitors. The knock came on the door, and my father told us to be quiet and keep packing. I thought it might have been Getzel or one of his boys to take what we were packing to the Nazis. I peeked down the stairwell and saw my father open the door. It was not Getzel, and it was not a soldier or any ruffian band of Ukrainians. In the door frame stood a man and a woman. They were well dressed, and she was very pretty, with blonde hair and blue eyes. He was tall and held his back straight and head high as if he were a nobleman. My father eyed them over quickly and invited them in.

I couldn't hear most of what my father and the strange man were saying to each other, and what I could hear I didn't understand. I watched my father's face change from confused to angry and then from angry to sad.

By the end of the conversation, I didn't know what had happened, but I knew it wasn't good. Something unsavory started churning in my stomach. My father saw the strangers out and closed the door, and I scampered off to attend to my packing once more.

Later that night, as we sat around the table for our final meal in our own home, my father told us about the strange visitors.

"A man and a woman came to our home today," he said, after swallowing a mouthful of bread.

"What did they want?" my mother asked.

"They brought news from the new authorities," he said. "He's some big shot principal. They are coming to take over our home. It is theirs now."

"What?" shouted my sister. Even when she was angry she was beautiful, with her blonde hair and her blue eyes. "How can this be? What right do they—"

"Channah!" my father interrupted. "Please, this is not easy for any of us. They have the German army behind them. The Nazis told them to pick any house. Of course, we Jews won't need our houses anymore. They will come tomorrow before we leave for the ghetto."

"Does that mean we won't be coming back?" I asked. "Ever?"

"We will cross that bridge when we get to it," my mother told me, placing her warm hand on my injured one.

My father looked at my mother then, and something twinkled in his eye. I hadn't seen that twinkle in months. It was only there for a moment, however, and then his face sagged again.

"Finish your supper," he told us. "Then go to sleep. We will have a long day tomorrow."

I knew they had picked our house because it was new and beautiful. My father had put everything he had into it. *Our* house. And now, easy as pie, like taking candy out of a baby's mouth, it was theirs.

The Offer

We were all ready to go in the morning when the principal, Mr. Lomtska, and his wife came. We had our boxes ready. We had said good-bye to the house. When Mrs. Lomtska saw us all standing there, my sister and I with tears in our eyes, my mother with her own cheeks red from crying, and my father, fallen, she didn't bother to show her emotion, but she did stare at my sister.

"You know," she began, "these children are just going to be killed in the ghetto."

My father looked at Mrs. Lomtska with a mixture of shock and anger. He held his tongue. I wondered if what she said was true, and my heart hit my throat. She continued to stare at Channah.

The principal cleared his throat and placed a hand on the back of his wife's neck.

"Just look at the older one," she continued, speaking to her husband. "Her hair is blonde, her eyes are blue. She doesn't look Jewish. And look how fiery she is; I can tell she is intelligent."

"Dear," the principal said, "they have to go with their parents. It's the law, I'm afraid."

"But we have no children of our own!" Mrs. Lomstka insisted. She put a hand on her husband's shoulder. "We could keep her and say she is ours. They're just going to be killed anyway."

The principal seemed to consider this. I couldn't believe what I was hearing, and I wondered if they could actually do that. And if they could, what would my parents say? There was a long while when the principal just stared at Channah. She was crying quietly. Mrs. Lomtska kept petting Mr. Lomtska on his shoulder, making a little whimpering sound, as if she were picking out a puppy. At last the principal said something.

"I suppose we could keep her," he said. "She does have blonde hair and blue eyes. She's very beautiful, actually. I'm quite impressed with her."

I didn't know what to say or think. My parents looked panicky, and Mrs. Lomtska was suddenly wide-eyed and smiling with delight.

"What do you say?" asked the principal.

"Absolutely not," said my father. "We are a family. If we go to the ghetto, we go as a family. What do you think this is? Who do you think you are? This is my daughter you are speaking about."

With that, my father stormed from the house, and we followed him.

The Ghetto and the Seeds of Fire

When we got to the area of town that was chained off to be the ghetto, our already deterred spirits died a little more. It was complete bedlam: the Nazis riding around, Jews being herded in, loudspeakers blaring messages that the gates would be closed in a week. For now, with the gate still open, people came and went as they pleased.

Despite the commotion, there was no panic. There was no feeling of any kind of urgency. There was only a very deep sense of some end, but it was not here yet so people just went on the way that they could.

Ukrainians walked around the borders of the ghetto carrying sacks, eyeing the ghetto and the Jewish people, waiting like locusts for the Jews to be killed so that they could plunder their goods.

It was a Saturday, I think, two days before Yom Kippur. Yom Kippur is one of two Jewish High Holidays, which means it's very important. It's a time when the Jewish people gather to say sorry for all their wrongdoings over the year, and they do this by fasting so that they can start fresh in the new year.

A few days before Yom Kippur we walked straight to my grandmother's house where my aunts and cousins were. It was sort of like just going to Grandma's, but I noticed on the way there the streets were very crowded. There was an uneasiness inside of everyone, an oily feeling that leaked out all over the place. It almost felt like we were going there for the holiday, but it didn't. It felt like we were going there for some other unknown purpose. I felt like an animal getting taken from the wild and being put in the zoo.

When we got to my grandmother's house, my father was very quiet. I remember trying to imagine what was happening in his head. It must have been terrible to watch everything he had ever worked for taken away, to watch his family in such danger, and he was powerless to stop it. My sister and I kept ourselves occupied, and my mother helped my father's sisters around the house. We were just waiting, waiting for what I don't know, but it definitely felt like waiting. My father was thinking. I saw that glimmer in his eye again, the one from the night before, and I knew that he was thinking. He only got that look when he thought about something very heavy or when he read the bible.

We weren't privy to the meeting that I'm about to tell you about. We didn't go to it, we didn't even know about it, but it's been recorded as historical fact. Later that night, Getzel and his boys, now inside of the ghetto, were at prayers with a large group of other Jews. Some of them had been on the Judenrat committee, and some of them were strong young men.

The Judenrat members, with whatever influence they had with the Nazis, managed to keep the ghetto gates opened this long. The Ukrainians had tried to have the doors closed as early as August 1942. The Judenrat even managed to keep them from building the fence that enclosed the ghetto until July and kept the gates open until the Nazis announced that the gates would be closing soon. All of this time, Getzel and his boys had not been idle. They had been meeting with young men and women, all kinds of activists. I mentioned earlier that the Gestapo would come to understand that forcing the Judenrat to commit horrific choices did not come without its price. The time had nearly come for action.

"Jews," Getzel must have said, or something like this in the midst of their prayers, "the dawn of our revolt is at hand. The plan is plain, but it is all we have. We are now caged like beasts. Let us break free of these boundaries. We built these homes. Now we will destroy them in the name of our G-d, Hashem. Let Him deliver us again from the bonds of slavery and murder!

"Pass the word to your neighbors that on our signal, everyone is to set his own house ablaze with fire. We have materials gathered from months of our underground work. Many young Jews died getting these supplies. We have five rifles, twenty-five pistols, a few hand grenades, and most importantly we have our fire. The time will be upon us soon. May G-d be with us."

I can imagine the people at that meeting were electrified, but terrified. I can imagine that in their hearts the fire had already started.

The Escape

I didn't have to wait long to discover what that twinkle in my father's eye had been about. The morning after we'd moved into the ghetto, Sunday, September 20, 1942, he gathered me, my mother, and Channah into a quiet room in my grandmother's house. He made sure that nobody else was listening.

"Pearl," my father said to my mother, "the other night, when Libe asked you if we would ever be going back to our home, what did you tell her?"

"I ... I ..." my mother stammered. She was a little confused. "I don't remember. I think I said that we would cross that bridge when we—"

"Yes!" said my father. "You said that we would cross a bridge. That gave me an idea, one that might save all our lives."

"What are you talking about?" my mother asked. She looked worried for him.

"Pavlo," he answered. "Girls, do you remember the man who came to us with food a long time ago when Libe and your mother were sick, healing in Grandma's house?"

We nodded.

"This man is an old business partner of mine," my father continued. "He is a good man—"

"He is Ukrainian!" said my mother.

"Pavlo is not like them," answered my father. "He is a good man! His farm is in the west, across the river. Listen, the gates are still open for now, but in a few days they will be closed. And then we will be killed!"

"We don't know that!" My mother was panicking. She was frightened.

"We do!" my father said angrily. "We'll leave immediately, take nothing with us. We'll leave the ghetto and cross the river. Pavlo will foster us. I know he will."

We all sat in quiet for a moment, soaking in my father's words. It was dangerous, it was risky, but he was right. It could save our lives. We agreed.

In the matter of an hour, we said good-bye to our grandmother and our aunts and anyone else who might have been staying in that house; I know there were others, I just don't quite remember who they were exactly. I laced up my tall brown boots and we were off, back into the streets of the ghetto, weaving around people who were not panicking, passing by houses that had become prisons, avoiding locking eyes with our fellow Jews, the very people who once made up our beautiful community but who now seemed like trapped souls wandering between two worlds.

We made it to the gates. I can remember thinking that the Nazis weren't going to let us through, but there was no problem. We simply left. It is so odd to think about that now, how we just walked out of the ghetto like that. It is hard to believe, but that's how it happened. So many things that happened during the Holocaust baffle any normal mind. Human nature can baffle any normal mind. But, as it was for many people, what saved us was luck.

It was three kilometers to Pavlo's farm. We were going to have to go west through Tuchin, cross the river Horyn, and then find his land on the other side. My father knew where it was from his business dealings, but he had no way to get word to Pavlo that we might be coming, and I knew that if we were caught trying to escape Tuchin, we would be killed on the spot. Leaving the ghetto was one thing because the gates hadn't closed yet. Escaping Tuchin and our ultimate fate, the one the Nazis had planned to deliver to us firsthand, would not be tolerated.

It was slow work, moving through the town and appearing that we were not going to flee. Eventually, we did make it to the river. It was a relief and a burden all at once. We had come close to escaping; however, there were no buildings near the river to hide us from the sight of any Nazi soldiers or, worse, any of the Ukrainians.

I remember there was a little boat on the river. We needed it to cross over. As fate would have it, there was a group of young Ukrainian boys by the boat, around thirteen or fourteen years old. There were six or seven of them. We were terrified, but we had no other options. My father approached the boys who were eyeing us with little smirks on their faces, like they had caught us and had us in their little paws.

"Hello, young men," said my father. I knew he must have been terrified, but his voice didn't show it.

"Jews!" said one of the youngsters. "You're supposed to be in the ghetto."

"Please," said my father hurriedly. "We have money. We need to get to the other side of the river. Our friend waits for us. Please keep quiet, and bring us across the river. I will pay you handsomely."

The boys joked about turning us over to an SS officer who they had seen riding by on a motorcycle earlier. I held onto my mother tightly, but we kept perfectly quiet. Finally, one of the boys waved us over to the boat.

"All right," he said. "Get in the boat, you stinking Jews. Give us the money and we'll take you across."

My father put his arm around my mother and guided us to the boat. The boys rocked it and laughed as we tried to get in.

"Come on," one of the boys said. "Hand over the money, now!"

My father complied. He looked worried for us, but I could see that he was trying very hard to keep his face from showing his anger. He handed the boy some money and everyone got into the boat. I had never been more nervous before in my life. Halfway across the river, one of the boys stood up on the boat and started to rock it violently back and forth, back and forth.

"Please!" my sister yelled.

"Shut up," said one of the boys, "or we'll call out for the Nazis. Dirty Jews! We think you need a bath!"

The Ukrainian boys all started to laugh at us and rock the boat even harder.

"I paid you the fare!" said my father. "Please keep going. Get us to the fields on the other side."

"You haven't paid *me* yet!" shouted one of the boys.

"Or me," said another.

In turn, each of the hoodlums demanded that my father pay them, and of course my father did. They slapped him around and rocked the boat. I cried and cried. They took all of his money. They brought me to tears and infuriated my sister. My mother's eyes I remember were empty, looking off far, far away somewhere.

The boys were horrible, but they got us to the other side of the river, and for a moment we were relieved. Our hearts felt lighter. The obstacle of the river had been vanquished, and it was only a short distance through the fields to Pavlo's house, but as soon as we landed on the shore, our hearts became heavy again. The Ukrainian boys started running and shouting for the Nazis.

"Help! Jews are escaping from the ghetto!"

"Stop the dirty Jews!"

"The filthy rats are running away! Help!"

Those boys kept us hostage for two hours. I could tell that my father was furious and that he wanted to destroy these boys, but we were powerless.

Sure enough, soon came the police. I knew that this was it. We were surely going to be killed here. The Nazi police came and started beating my father. I hid my face in my mother's clothes and my sister shouted for them to stop, but it was not over. All of a sudden an SS officer on a motorcycle came riding up to us, probably the same officer the Ukrainian boys had seen earlier.

"What is going on here?" asked the SS officer.

"These Jews are trying to escape," said one of the Nazis. "We are beating them."

For a moment, I thought that the SS officer would get off of his motorcycle and assist the police in beating my father. He looked around at the whole scenario, and our eyes met. At first I saw a terrible thing: a man without a heart and eyes to match, with no soul behind them. I saw a well-built machine that was following a system of rules, and those rules just happened to involve destroying me and my family. Then something divine happened. I saw a faltering, a melting of the slightest amount. His eyes were upon mine for just a fraction of a second, but I saw the tiniest hint of a human peek out from behind those cold, steel eyes of his. He looked at my sister and me. He looked at my tears and our clothes. He looked at my boots, with all of those laces.

"Well, stop it," said the SS officer finally. "Send them back to the ghetto with the rest of the filth."

It was in that strange way that an SS officer actually saved us, or at least my father, from being beaten to death. In my mind, though, there was no celebration. We were going back to the ghetto. We were going to our graves anyway.

The Lucky Colors

In a matter of hours, we were back at my grandmother's house, back in the ghetto. It had all been for nothing. We were downtrodden and resigned. My father and mother had decided they would do the only thing they knew could help anyone. They were going to save my sister. They had decided to take her to live with the principal and his wife, the Lomtskas. The Lomtskas were childless and they would adopt her. She could pass for a gentile with her blue eyes and blonde hair. Channah was chosen to live.

"It is luck that she should have her looks," said my mother to me. "She will get to live because of them."

"Don't go," I told Channah, as my parents dressed her up in fine clothes and fixed her hair. I'll never forget that my mother tied two big bright red bows into her hair, bows that inspired sounds of low-flying airplanes in my head. "Don't go."

I had a terrible feeling that those would be the last words I would have a chance to say to my sister for a very long time.

"I'll do what Mama and Papa say," she replied.

When she was ready, I ran to cry in a dark bedroom, but I heard my father speaking to her before he left to take her to our old house, to the principal and his wife.

"Channah," he said, "before they close the gates, come back and say good-bye to the family. We'll want to see you one last time."

"What will happen when they close the gates, Father?" she asked.

"One day, Channah," he said, avoiding her question, "we will get you back, and we will reunite."

Then they were gone. I remember that evening was the start of Yom Kippur, and I remember whispering into the pillow, wet with my salty tears: "Don't go. Don't go." But she left to be saved when we stayed to die. What can I say? She had the lucky colors.

Pavlo Ashamed

The night was miserable. My father had come back in less than an hour without my sister. It was a quiet time in the ghetto. It was not the time for worship or atonement. The air was heavy with rumors and wild theories. This was when the panic began.

Jews came and went into each other's houses, all of us trying to find out what was going on. Some said that the Nazis were digging trenches near the railway station. We knew this to mean grave sites. Others said that they were going to close the gates earlier than previously reported. It was one horrible thing after the other. The mood was awful. We were wallowing in our sorrow when out of the blue sky arrived a surprise visitor to my grandmother's house. Pavlo, the farmer, was back.

He sat with my father.

"I heard through the village that you tried to come to our farm," he said. His voice was deep and powerful, but his eyes were gentle and warm. He was the kind of man you felt safe with. But he was a poor Ukrainian farmer with a big family, a nice grain business, and a lot to lose.

"Why have you come?" my father asked.

"I am ashamed," said Pavlo, and his eyes fell to the floor.

"Of what? You have done nothing," assured my father.

"I am ashamed of my people," said the poor farmer. "I am disgusted by what is happening here. Do you know what is to happen to the people in this place? Do you know what is to happen to *you*? I've come to help."

My family sat in silence.

"Do you realize how much danger you have put yourself in just by coming here?" my father quietly asked his old business friend. "Not to mention the risk you will take if you try to help us escape. We have already gotten caught once."

"I can't take you, Isaak," Pavlo said. "But I can take your wife and your girls. We will dress them up as peasants. I have thought about this."

"My eldest daughter is already safe," said my father. I could see the pain in his eyes as he said those words aloud, reminding him that he would probably never see her again. But he sighed some slight relief, knowing she would remain alive even if he would not.

"That is better," said Pavlo. "It will be easier to maneuver unnoticed with only Pearl and Libe. I can claim that Pearl is my wife and that Libe is my daughter if I am stopped."

Pavlo paused and looked at me. His eyes were wet, and they sparkled as he shook his head slowly back and forth.

"What did this child do to deserve this?" he asked to no one, for of course no one had an answer.

My father sighed and rubbed his temples.

"I don't know what to say," he breathed.

"You don't have to say anything," said Pavlo. "I am only doing what anyone should. You are a good man, Isaak. You would do the same for my family."

My father nodded, stood, and clapped Pavlo on the shoulder.

"We will never forget this," he said.

It was difficult to say good-bye to my father. I had already seen my sister go, and now I was leaving him. It was the hardest thing I had been forced to do so far in our living nightmare. Thank goodness I had my mother with me. I don't know if I could have gone with Pavlo, leaving the both of them behind. Still, it was terrible.

It was day when we left; Pavlo, my mother, and I left my grandmother's house and found our way through the tense streets of the ghetto. All I had were the clothes on my back, my tall boots with the many laces, and a distant memory of the sounds of airplanes and red ribbons in my hair.

The Ghetto Besieged

I t was luck once more that my mother and I were gone. We had left with Pavlo, but I learned of what I am about to tell you many years later; it's all in the history books.

It was a Tuesday when the Nazis rounded up the rest of the Jews in the area and forced them into the ghetto. They were going to close the gates early. It was a surprise to all of the Jews who were still in the ghetto, including my father. Getzel Schwartzman and his resistance began gathering at structures near the gates. My father had other plans.

SS soldiers came into the town that day, and they formed a barrier around the ghetto. Himmerlfarb, who worked with Getzel and had been part of the Judenrat, helped gather the resistance and went around the ghetto warning everyone of what was about to happen.

Do you remember me telling you that there was no panic in the ghetto? It was true. But when the second the SS unit arrived, the moment they closed the gates, there was chaos. There was fear beyond what those Jews had known before. There was panic.

The people in the ghetto had sat in their cage with the lock undone and the door swung open, and they were weary, but they were content to sit. The moment that door closed and the lock snapped shut, something had transformed and there was chaos!

Simply put, the Jews had hoped. We had believed, wrongly in this case, but we had believed that people wouldn't, couldn't do the things we had heard about them doing. We believed in humankind. We knew what was going to happen, but we refused to believe it, not because we were ignorant, but because we were people. That is why the Jews stayed until it was too late.

In the very early hours on Thursday, September 24, 1942, the Jews set fire to their homes. The Gestapo marched upon the ghetto along with the Ukrainian police, firing their weapons, shouting their orders. They came to kill all of the Jews.

My father would have stayed to fight, but he knew my sister was planning on coming to the ghetto later that morning to say good-bye to the family, and so he had already gone, before the fire started. He said his good-byes to his sisters, my aunts; his parents; and then ran into the streets. His plan was to escape and find my sister before she would come and be killed.

The ghetto was dry and ripe for flame. The Jews of Tuchin began their revolt.

III. A Dark Light in Tuchin

Pavlo's Farm

Before the uprising in the ghetto began, my mother and I made our journey with Pavlo. Since we were with him and were dressed as peasants, and there was so much for the Nazis to do at the time, we had no trouble moving through Tuchin. We walked the whole way. We saw a few soldiers here and there, but there was nothing that hindered us.

The three kilometers took us a little less than an hour to cover. I was terrified that when we crossed the river, we would again be caught, but nothing happened while we traveled with Pavlo. I thought of my sister and my father, and I wondered if I would ever see them again. I thought of my dolly in the pot, in the basement of the home that was no longer ours. I thought of Pavlo.

I began to consider this man. Here was a man, a Ukraine, who was risking his life, his family, and his livelihood for us. Who were we to him? My father's family, that's all. We were practically strangers. Pavlo was a tall man. He looked like a plain ordinary farmer. He had a great big forehead, the kind that was perfect for thinking, a pointed nose, with eyes close to it, and hollowed, well-defined cheek bones. He looked like a serious man, but his warmth and quiet nature let us know that he wasn't stern. And his actions let us know he wasn't a man at all; he was an angel among men.

Pavlo led us in near silence the whole way to his farm. As we approached his house, we passed cows and haystacks, a little barn by a wooden fence, a few pigs, some goats, scattered scraggly looking trees, and I thought I heard the sound of a dog barking somewhere on the other side of his land. His house was white with a wooden roof and an attic. There were windows on the right side, and there was an awning near the front doors.

When we arrived it was evening, and Pavlo's entire family was absent. His wife, Lubka, was not there; neither were their three teenage children: Klavdiya, Galina, and Nikolay. Pavlo's brother and a woman who might have been another relative also lived on the farm at the time, and they were not there either. Whether this was by some design of Pavlo's or a lucky chance, I cannot say.

When we walked in, I felt like we had just ruined their household by stepping into it. It felt very alien to us, like we were intruding on some holy ground. But Pavlo eased my discomfort.

"It will be safe here tonight," Pavlo said.

My mother nodded.

I wanted to sit down at the kitchen table; we were hungry from our journey. Instead, Pavlo took us to a bedroom.

"You will stay here," Pavlo told us. "You must be ready to run at any sign of the soldiers. My brother has no idea that I am hiding you here. It is very dangerous for us. If I am caught hiding Jews, they will treat my family as Jews and we will all be killed. Hopefully, this commotion will pass quickly. I will be by soon with some food for you both. After that, it would be best if you could try to get some sleep."

My mother thanked him, but I just stared at the roof, worrying. I thought of my boots and how they had so many laces. I wondered if I would be able to lace them all up in time ... if we had to run.

Out of the Fire, Over the Fence, and Under the Stairs

I can imagine that while my father ran through the streets of the ghetto in Tuchin in the still hum before the beginning of the revolt, during the very early hours on September 24, sometime around 3:30 in the morning, the Jews would soon be shouting the alarm that they were all about to be killed.

When my father made it to the fence, he saw that it was swarmed by young Jewish men furiously attempting to climb over. They had succeeded in ruining the fence in certain areas, but most of these people were being shot immediately by the Nazis.

Like so many others, he took a running start and attempted to leap over. By some manner of luck, an officer must have sneezed or was distracted by a fly or he noticed some other Jews trying to escape. It was nothing short of a miracle that in the midst of the disorder, my father was able to escape over the fence and not get shot in the head. Unlike so many others that morning, my father made it over. It was a blessing that my father moved past the Nazis and the Ukrainian skinheads who had their bags ready to loot.

After he had gone, the first fire was lit. By this time a good deal of the fence was down and Getzel shouted for the Jews to flee. Someone had lit his home on fire, and that was the signal. The rest followed. The scrambling Jews would soon feel the heat and smell the smoke as they moved through the ghetto. The flames and rifles crackled and cracked. The soldiers barked and hollered. The Jews belted their response.

The Gestapo and the Ukrainians charged the ghetto and the Jews fought them with any might or weapon they could muster.

Farther and farther away from the revolt, my father fled. He ran through Tuchin all the way back to our home where he sought my sister. My father left the ghetto and the resisters behind, silently praying for them.

I can't really imagine what my father must have felt as he approached the house he had built, given the circumstances of its current owners and the state of Tuchin, but I'm sure that he was relieved to see his daughter. My sister, Channah, was just about to leave for the ghetto when my father arrived, and the timing had been lucky once again. It probably seemed to my father, at the time anyway, that my sister was a very lucky girl.

The principal and his wife were standing by the side of the house with my sister when my father arrived.

"Channah!" shouted my father.

"Papa!"

They embraced.

"But what are you doing here?" Mr. Lomtska asked my father. "We were about to escort Channah to say farewell to your family."

"The ghetto is burning. Look." My father pointed to the sky behind the house where plumes of dark smoke could be seen against the bright morning sky.

"My goodness!" Mrs. Lomtska gasped.

"Listen," said my father, thinking quickly. "I must return to the ghetto, but I only came to warn Channah not to come. I will be caught and killed if I attempt to escape. I only came to say good-bye. May I please have a moment alone with my daughter?"

"Of course," said Mr. Lomtska, and the principal and his wife went back into the house, leaving my sister and father alone.

My father embraced Channah again. There must have been tears in her eyes as she imagined the worse for the people in the ghetto, including the rest of her family.

"Channah," he whispered hurriedly. "Listen closely. Your mother and sister are safe. They are with Pavlo at his farm. Listen, Channah, stop crying. I need you to pay close attention."

"Please, Papa," she begged. "Don't go back to the ghetto. You will be killed."

"I am not," he answered. "Listen to me. Do you remember when I showed you the secret about our stairs in the house? The underneath part?"

Channah nodded.

"I'm going to hide there," he told her. He grabbed his daughter's shoulders. "And I need you to pretend to the principal and his wife that I returned to the ghetto. And I'll need you to bring me food when you can. Do you understand?"

"Yes!" she answered, probably still weeping.

My father kissed my sister on the cheek and disappeared under the house as she went back inside to lie to her new parents so that she could help save our father's life.

Getzel Schwartzman

Two thousand Jews escaped from the burning ghetto and ran into the forest in the north, the very same forest where I once hid under a tree, worrying that my red ribbons would alert the Russian airplanes of our presence. The rest of the Jews, one thousand Jewish people, were either killed by Nazis or the very fire that the Jews themselves had started. The revolt at Tuchin lasted well into Friday, September 25, 1942. The Jews managed to take some of the Nazis down, and even a couple of Ukrainians. However, the sad truth is, out of those two thousand Jews who managed to evade bullets and flame, none of them actually survived.

In the forest, the Jews were hunted. They were caught and killed by Ukrainians. Three hundred women and their babies who couldn't stand being in the forest eventually returned to the town. The Nazis had promised that they would be able to live in the ghetto once the fires stopped. Instead, these three hundred Jews were immediately shot by those Nazis, those liars, those men without hearts.

Getzel and the other remaining survivors in the ghetto decided to give themselves up on Saturday, September 26.

"We were the organizers of this revolt!" Getzel announced, proud of the Jews' stance at the ghetto. "I only ask that I be allowed to die in the Jewish cemetery!"

The Nazis were pleased to oblige Getzel's request, and they shot him dead in the Tuchin graveyard.

Light in the Dark

The second night that we were at Pavlo's, he moved us to the attic. He brought us food. On the night of September 25, as the ghetto burned, my mother and I stared out of a tiny window in the attic wall. Pavlo sat with us.

"This is a terrible sign," Pavlo said. "You will not be able to leave here now."

My mother's eyes began to tear. She was probably thinking of my father like I was. I held her hand.

The three of us stared. The night was black, but within the darkness there burned a single glowing gash on the horizon, a blood-red slash with a golden center broken by streaks of pitch-black smoke, like the claw marks of a tiger. I looked at my mother's eyes, and they twinkled with teardrops and faraway fire. I was frightened. I felt like I had been buried alive after all.

IV. Brisko

One Week

For seven days and seven nights my sister kept my father alive in the hole under the stairs. At supper, she would wait until the principal and his wife were involved in some conversation and not paying attention to her, then she would sneak a piece of bread or whatever was on the table and slip it into her sleeve. It was very dangerous because Channah could have been caught by the principal, and if that had been the case she could have been beaten or, worse, turned over to the Nazis.

If not for Channah's bravery, though, my father would not have survived.

She would come out of the house quietly after dark and go to the staircase on the side of the house. There, Channah would remove the middle stair and whisper down to our father. He would take the bread and thank his daughter. Thank goodness they weren't caught, not by the principal, not by the Ukrainian neighbors, and not by the Nazis. It was all luck how this worked out.

After a week, my father knew that he could not continue surviving in that condition. He knew what risk he was putting Channah at, and he wanted to make sure that my mother and I had reached Pavlo's farm, that we were safe. So it was that after seven days of harboring my father under what used to be his own staircase, my sister said good-bye to him and said a prayer for him as he left for Pavlo's farm.

My father told my sister that when the war was over, they would reunite and that they should look for each other when the time was right.

The Sinking Weather Shines on Us

B y the time my father arrived at the farm, we had been there for about a week hiding in the attic. Pavlo's wife was ready for us to leave. Pavlo was on edge, understandably. It was just as frightening for him as it was for us. Everyone's lives were at stake, not just ours.

You can imagine, then, that when my father showed up at the farm, Pavlo was not pleased. He was surprised.

"Isaak, I was not expecting you," Pavlo said to my father inside of the house. My mother and I came down from the attic to greet him. "You and your family will have to leave here."

"Pavlo ..." my father began, but he knew he could not argue with the man who had already saved his family's life.

"I am afraid," Pavlo continued. "I have three children. I have my wife to think about. We don't have the food to feed your family. I'm just a poor farmer! Take your wife and daughter and go."

Pavlo's voice was shaky. I could tell that he meant what he said, but only with his mind. His heart, on the other hand, was screaming. He looked at me.

"We will go, of course," said my father softly.

"What did this child do to deserve this?" Pavlo breathed, still looking at me. I knew then that he wouldn't let us leave. At that moment, the wind picked up. The house shook, and fresh snow splattered on the window.

Pavlo looked outside and sighed. We all waited with stayed breath and beating hearts. I wanted to hug Pavlo and take his worry away. Somewhere outside a dog whimpered, or it could have been the wind.

"Isaak," Pavlo started again, "go with your family upstairs for now. This weather is no good for travel. It is cold enough for Libe to freeze to death. You'll stay in the attic tonight, but when the weather clears tomorrow, you must go."

"Thank you, Pavlo," my father said, and he reached into his pocket and took out a gold watch that I remembered my mother used to wear before the war. "Please take this as payment."

Pavlo stared at the watch, and then reached out and grabbed it.

"I will hold onto this watch for you, my friend," he told my father. "But when this war is over, it will be yours again."

We went quietly, somberly back upstairs. My mother embraced my father like I had never seen her cling to anyone before. I stared out the window and watched the snow thicken and fall. I wished with all my might that for one moment I could forget about the Nazis and the war, that I could go outside and enjoy the snow like a normal child. I fell asleep to that thought, and I may have even had a dream.

The next day Pavlo did make us leave the attic, but he did not kick us off of his farm. He moved us outside to a haystack that he had hollowed out. I remember feeling very much like my little dolly, thrown into the cold pot in our basement.

It was cold and cramped. There was a dog that would run around in the field barking loudly. He was a big dog, something like a mutt, with black and brown fur, a long nose, and a pair of short, floppy ears. There was something about the dog running around that took away some of my sadness. There was something normal about seeing a dog. There was also something very extraordinary about that particular dog, but I didn't know yet what it was.

Before Pavlo stopped up the opening in the haystack, which we had crawled through to get inside, he leaned in closely.

"I will bring you food when I can," he said. "You must not make any sounds or leave here. The Nazis have been searching the village for escaped Jews. You should be safe here if you stay quiet. Not even my brother knows you are here. Please, stay put. Do not endanger my family."

His face was severe; he looked stressed.

"I'm afraid," I managed to say before he closed us in with more hay. The dog let out a bark.

"Do you hear that?" Pavlo asked me. "That is my dog. His name is Brisko, and he will not let anything bad happen to you." Pavlo managed a smile. Then he piled up the rest of the hay and everything was dark.

"Brisko ...." I whispered, and somehow felt just a little warmer.

The Boots
and the Bark

This was the beginning of our new life, the start of our real test. The torment began here. For the next eighteen months, yes, for eighteen months we would be hiding. There are twelve months in a year. Six months is a half of a year. Eighteen months is one year plus another half of a year. It is an incredibly long time to be doing any one thing—but to hide, and in the conditions that we had to survive in ...

For the first two months we lived in a hole in the ground, in a haystack outside, in the winter. Not for a few days. Not for a few weeks. We lived in a hole in the ground, in a haystack, outside, in the winter, for two months. I repeat myself not because I think you don't understand but because it is so hard to imagine what this was like for someone who hasn't experienced it. If you want to get an idea of what I'm talking about, try to crawl into a dark tight spot. You can go underneath your desk, your bed, into your closet, anywhere. Just make sure that you cannot stand up or turn around. Make sure that you cannot see the light of day in the middle of the afternoon. Make sure that you don't have food or water or a place to go to the bathroom. Stay there for eight minutes. Now, imagine that those eight minutes were really eight weeks.

We were in the haystack for two months. Pavlo would sneak out to bring us pieces of bread, once a day if we were lucky. I don't remember how we took care of our excrement. I only remember that we never left that haystack for two months. We were cramped and bored. We could not make any noises. And the worst part was that Pavlo was not mistaken about the Nazis conducting raids on local farms. They came, and they came often.

Schnell! Schnell! Schnell! Hurry! Hurry! Hurry! That was in my thoughts and in my dreams. I was terrified. I was horrified all of my waking hours, and I was haunted during sleep, when I could manage that. I was so afraid that the Nazis would find us, and that when they did, they would be angry. They would be so mad that they would have to wait for me to come out. They would tell my mother and my father to come out, and I was terrified that I would be so slow because of my boots. I would be sitting there, lacing up my tall brown boots, and they would be furious that I was taking too long. So I constantly thought about lacing up my boots. I would practice lacing them up, and the whole time I would hear them shouting at me: *Schnell! Schnell! Schnell!* Hurry! Hurry! Hurry!

Of all the worries in the world, my boots were at the top of my list. They haunted me. It was such a simple thing, but it had so much terrifying weight behind it, so many scary consequences.

Schnell! Schnell! Schnell!

With the three of us in the hole, there was barely space to move. The air was stale. It was freezing cold. For two months, we lived like this. How we survived, I have no idea.

The Nazis were constantly coming onto the farm. But we always had a warning. Brisko knew what was happening. That dog was very smart. He knew that the Nazis were looking for us. He knew that the Nazis wanted to end our lives, and he knew that if he tried to protect us, they would kill him. The dog risked his life to save ours. We would hear Brisko barking first to warn us. Then we'd hear the boots stomping across the ground, and Pavlo would speak to the Nazis, show them around the farm. I remember thinking when they came that it was finally time, things were over. I would grab my boots and lace, lace, lace.

Brisko's bark was the only warning we ever had. He knew what he was doing.

When the Nazis weren't there, we were terrified, too. All I can remember thinking was that I wished I was anything else in the world but me. I hated being me while we lived in the haystack. I wished I was anything but a little Jewish girl. When I heard a bird chirp in the distance, I wanted to be a bird. When I heard Brisko bark, I wanted to be a dog. I wanted to be a non-Jew, anything, even a cat, so that I could just sit outside without being afraid that I was going to get killed. Such a simple thought, just the idea of sitting outside on a step somewhere without being afraid that I was going to get killed for being a Jew. It's a terrible feeling, not wanting to be who you are.

But I didn't have time for those fanciful thoughts when the Germans came around the farm. My mind would fixate on my boots. There were just so many laces.

Brisko's bark saved me in times of danger and times of boredom. He brought us warning and kept my imagination alive. He chose to play in front of our haystack because he knew that I needed him.

Despite Brisko's protection, eventually the Nazis started coming to the farms prepared. They were learning the little tricks people used to hide in creative places, such as haystacks. So they started coming to Pavlo's farm with these huge metal poles. They were sharp on one end so that they could pierce through condensed packs of hay and dig around to find any people who might be hiding within.

After a few months of us living in conditions worse than a prison, the Nazis started to come to Pavlo's farm with these poles, and we knew that our time was almost up. No matter how fast I could lace my boots, no matter how loud Brisko would bark, nothing could hide us from those poles. Yet time and time again, they came and searched and we were not found.

One day when they were stabbing through our haystack and Brisko was running around barking somewhere outside, the pole scratched my father's cheek. It was only a scratch, and it wasn't even enough for the German soldier to feel that he had hit something, but it left a little mark on his face. If that pole had been just a fraction of a centimeter to one direction, we would have been caught and killed. We knew in our hearts that day that it was the distraction of Brisko that moved that pole away from my father. It was too lucky. If the dog had not been barking at those soldiers, they would have had more time and more concentration. They would have found us.

After that incident, Pavlo knew we could no longer stay in the haystack. It was too dangerous. So for the first time in two months we left the haystack and moved into our final hiding place. This place would come to be the very center of the world for over a year. It was the center of the universe. It was where everything good and bad ever happened. It was heaven and life, it was nowhere, it was everywhere, and it was death. And I will never forget how it had been Brisko's mighty bark that had delivered us there.

How Tomorrow Never Came

oor Pavlo. For the entire time we had been in the haystack, he had been thinking of his wife and family. He was knowingly putting them all in danger, not to mention himself. He was taking food out of his children's mouths and giving it to us. And after our close encounter with the Nazis' poles, the tension was higher than ever. Every day that we spent in that haystack, and every day after, he came to us and told us that tomorrow we would have to leave the farm. Tomorrow never came.

Logically, he knew that we could not stay there, but his heart never let him enforce what his mind believed to be true. Pavlo would make all sorts of excuses to allow us to stay just one more day. It was mostly the weather.

"You won't be able to leave today after all," he would say. "The weather is much too frigid. You will have to wait for tomorrow."

Tomorrow never came. Pavlo would look at me and shake his head every time, always with tears in his eyes, and he would wonder aloud what this child (talking about me) could have possibly done to have deserved this. The answer was always nothing.

So when Pavlo realized the dangers of keeping us hidden in the haystack, he decided to move us into the barn. This would prove to be no less dangerous, no less torturous of a place to hide. The barn once housed horses, but Pavlo moved them out in order to hide us there. There was concrete in the middle of the barn, and there was hay stacked up high on either side of that. The hay that was against the slatted wooden wall would become our new home. Pavlo dug a little tunnel in that hay all the way to the wall and hollowed out a section that was maybe a few feet high and few feet wide. It was an incredibly small space for two adults and one child to live in for the remainder of those eighteen months, but of course we had no choice.

Even when we were in the barn, when Pavlo came to sneak us bread, once a day if we were lucky, he would tell us that tomorrow would be the day we would have to leave. Tomorrow never came. That didn't stop us from worrying that it would. We worried we'd be asked to leave, and of course my father wouldn't be able to argue. After all, Pavlo and his dog had already saved our lives. But we were terrified that once we left the farm, we'd be hunted and tracked, and found and killed. We were worried about the Nazis, yes, but we were more worried about the Ukrainians, the skinhead groups of Ukrainians especially.

Those Ukrainians were the ones who had hunted down the Jews who fled from the Tuchin ghetto into the forest. They were the ones who had led the pogram. These Ukrainians would say, "A bullet is too good for a Jew," so instead they would cut them up into pieces.

But that worry would not come to pass for us. Pavlo never made us leave the farm. Because of his heart, because he loved us, and for no other reason than we were fellow humans who did not deserve what was happening to us, tomorrow never came.

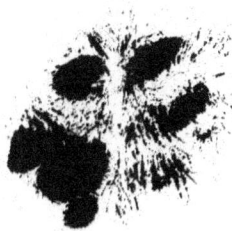

Through the Barn Slats

Although tomorrow never came, *today* was always with us. We could never escape the present. Eighteen months was a long time to sit around with nothing at all to occupy our minds.

We stayed in the part of the hay that was against the wall and hollowed out, but it was very small. My father was constantly in a bending position. Because I was a child, I was the only one who could sit properly, but even I couldn't stand. My mother was petite, so she didn't have to bend as much as my father did. I can't imagine what my father felt like, always bending that whole time. But it was what we had to do, you know, to live.

It was so cramped inside of that barn that when one of us wanted to shift positions, we all had to turn around at the same time. We would do this from time to time to keep from stiffening up. I can still see my father's bent head if I close my eyes tightly enough. The whole thing was made even more difficult because for the eighteen months that we spent hiding on the farm, we wore the same clothes. There was no washing our hands or our faces. We must have stunk like pigs.

Mostly, we thought about my sister, Channah. We talked about her a lot, and we were thankful that she was alive and safe.

"When this is all over," my father would say, "we'll find Channah, and she will be ours again. At least she is living better than we are."

The only way that we could get any food while hiding in the barn was if Pavlo could sneak away from the house and get it to us. This was extremely dangerous, and there was a very special process that would happen in order to ensure Pavlo's safety and our safety. If Pavlo didn't follow this process, we would all have been killed for sure. There was one key element in this whole procedure, and that was Brisko, the dog. I'm telling you, that dog saved our lives over and over again. And he did it on purpose.

The whole time that we had been in the haystack, I never touched Brisko. He had been like a shadow, like some invisible alarm that made us all alert when trouble was around. Brisko had been untouchable, but he had been seen and known.

Like I said before, he was some mutt, spotted brown and black. He was not a purebred anything. He was just a mangy mutt. People are always putting so much stock in a good thoroughbred dog. Not me; I never will. I know that the mutts have the real *hutzpah*, or fire in the belly! Maybe, ironically, Brisko was part German shepherd. Maybe it was that he shared a history with the enemy. But whatever his body was made of, his soul was more important. And no one in the world can tell me that dogs don't have souls because Brisko's was brilliant, and I saw it every day through the barn slats.

To this day, I can cry thinking about that dog, what would have happened if he hadn't been as smart as he was or as loyal to Pavlo, or if he hadn't existed on that farm at all. But he had existed, thank goodness. Throughout time, dogs have proven to be amazing allies to humans, especially in times of great need. Brisko was no exception to this rule.

You know, there is one thing that all of the survivors from the Holocaust have in common and that is luck. Pure luck. Brisko was our luck; he was our hope. And I know it in my heart that he delivered us safely through the torrential storm of the Nazis.

When Pavlo thought that no one would be around, when he thought it was the safest moment to bring us food, he would put on his giant brown coat that had these huge deep pockets, and he would walk outside. I can remember watching through the slats of the barn, my only window to the world for those long months, watching Pavlo's tall figure saunter carefully in the cold, down from his house and into the field behind the barn. There he would stand straight-backed and whistle this powerful, mesmerizing echo of a whistle and then wait. In a few moments we would hear Brisko's paws padding across the field and his panting breaths. Brisko would run to his master and sit by him, waiting patiently for instructions. Pavlo would bend down and whisper something—we never knew what it was—into Brisko's floppy ear. I remember distinctly their silhouettes against the moon, and that would fill me with anticipation, some kind of excitement.

The dog would give the farmer a kiss, a good wet lick on the cheek, and then he'd dash off and away. Brisko would run all over the farm, barking the whole time, sniffing and scouring, searching, with the utmost sense of duty and loyalty. He searched for anyone, any sign of any stranger that might be nearby. Brisko was looking for Nazis, for Pavlo's neighbors, for Ukrainians, for anyone, even Pavlo's brother! No one was to know we were there. And if we were lucky enough that the dog didn't find anybody, Brisko would run back to his master and perform the last part of the ritual. If the coast was clear, Brisko would stand up on his hind two legs, looking more like a hairy man than a dog, and would lean his paws against Pavlo's chest. This became a great symbol for me. This dog became my hope. When he put his paws onto Pavlo's heart, we knew that we would be getting food. We knew that the Nazis were not on the farm, that no one else was there, and we knew then we would be able to survive until the next morning. Brisko, our deliverer.

Pavlo would accept Brisko's good job with a pat on the head, and then he would proceed to the barn where he would bring us a couple of scraps of bread out of those deep pockets in his coat. Now remember how poor Pavlo was and that these scraps of bread weren't leftovers; they were scraps he was taking out of his own mouth, his own children's mouths. Pavlo and Brisko, our angels!

On many nights we got no bread. That was because Pavlo never received the go-ahead from Brisko. The dog would find something suspicious and simply continue to run around and bark and never come back with the symbol of hope. On those nights, I was full of depression and fear. On those nights, something darker than the sky held back our angels.

When Pavlo would come into our barn, even with the extreme measures that he took with Brisko, there was still the chance that something could go wrong. So when Pavlo came, he always had some excuse. He was always there for some other purpose, like to get hay for the horses or something commonplace like that. That was in case Brisko had somehow managed to miss someone on the farm, and Pavlo would appear like he was doing something besides bringing food to the Jews hiding in his barn.

Elimination, that was another thing. We had no chance to go to a bathroom the whole of those eighteen months. Instead, all we had was a pot in which to do our business. Once a night, Pavlo would come out to the barn, whistle for Brisko, and if the farm was clear, Pavlo removed one of the slats on the outside wall next to where we stayed. This was the most dangerous part of it all. When the slat was removed, my father crawled out with our pot, and he and Pavlo walked to a little river where my father would empty the pot. This was also an opportunity for Pavlo to catch my father up on any news of the war, but they spoke rarely and quietly for fear of being overheard.

Well, you can imagine that during these eighteen months with no washing, wearing the same clothes, and in such a cramped space, we were filthy. We had lice all the time. It was horrible, but we got used to it. And the little scraps of bread that we ate, we had to share those with the mice, which were everywhere. In the beginning I was terrified of them, but like the lice, I simply got used to them. The mice would steal pieces of our bread, but we guarded any water we had with our all our might because it was only enough to really wet our lips with.

That's how it was in the barn. That's how we lived for over a year and a half. After 3:00 in the afternoon, it was dark. The light would no longer seep into the barn. I would look out and just see darkness. I often wondered, while sitting within that pocket of hay, in the darkness, in the barn, on the farm, how much deeper we would have to go. How much more I would be able to bear. The more we had to carry, it seemed, the more I was able to.

That was my life for those eighteen months, and the only thing that ever broke that up, the only glimmer of hope I ever saw, was through those barn slats: Brisko, the dog, defying his nature and standing up, leaning his two paws onto Pavlo's chest and telling everyone that, at least for now, all would be well.

The Song of Sanity

Eighteen months to lie there in silence would have dried up our brains. You know that saying, "If you don't use it, you lose it"? That's true. My father didn't want my brain to dry up, so there were little exercises that he would make me do. Mostly, we would recite the bible.

We prayed all the time. There was one prayer that I said with my father every night. It was the prayer for protection. Brisko seemed to be our answer to that prayer.

I always had the bedtime prayers singing in my head. That kept me sane. My father prayed and quoted the bible to me all day long. When he wasn't quoting, I was singing other songs in my head, songs we used to sing openly on the streets of Tuchin. I remember one song about a little boat that flew a blue and white flag. *Shata, shata, shata ...* I don't remember exactly how it went, but it was a Hebrew song, and I remember that the boat was floating.

I thought about the streets of Tuchin a lot during those eighteen months. I remembered playing and laughing with my sister. I thought of all the Jewish businesses and the way life used to be when all of the families would make their cholent, a slow-cooked brisket stew. We'd start the stew on Friday night before Shabbos, and it would cook until the next night. It was a practice that dated back to the Second Temple. But no one was making *cholent* in Tuchin anymore.

Anyway, that's how we stayed alive mentally—holding onto memories, reciting the bible, singing songs quietly or in our minds. I became very religious. My father practically taught me the entire bible while we hid in the hay. He was very concerned about my mind. It was good that he was. He saved my brain with what he did. And that was not all my father was doing in the barn. He also made shoes. That's right, shoes. He sat there and carved shoes out of wood. I don't know how Pavlo managed to get a couple of tools into the barn; maybe they had already been there. But my father worked on those shoes all day long, among the lice and the mice and the crouching and the cold.

My mother knitted beautiful sweaters. Again, I don't know how these materials were given to us. I just remember it happening. My parents would create these extraordinary things—the shoes, the sweaters, and they'd give them to Pavlo for his family. It was our only way to give back.

One night, when my father had come back from dumping the pot in the river with Pavlo, he had a smile on his face. It was strange to see that.

"Pavlo's daughters are a hot topic at their church," he told us. "It seems that everyone would like to know where they got their beautiful sweaters and shoes!"

Pavlo, of course, had made up some story to explain it away, but in that moment we had ourselves a private laugh. Yes, our lives were terrible during those eighteen months, but with Pavlo and Brisko's help, we were able to survive! That was the key, to just keep going. And we were going. We were going pretty well, considering our circumstances. Every day, when Pavlo would come to tell us that we didn't have to leave, with some excuse like bad weather, we counted our lucky stars. And we were lucky, relatively. We were lucky, considering. We *were*, until the Nazis came.

V. The Men Without Hearts and the Pheonix Rising

Six Black Weeks and
a Little Secret

I t was late in March. The year was 1944, and the war would soon be over. The German soldiers were on the run. They were in retreat in many areas, including in Ukraine. The tide had finally begun to turn against the Nazis. We had reached Pavlo's farm in late September of 1942. It had been the worst eighteen months of my life, the worst months of many lives.

But it got worse. Can you believe it? I would not believe it if I hadn't lived it, but this is what happened. When a group of Nazi soldiers were retreating from elsewhere in Ukraine, they came our way, and because of our location, because of the river and the lay of Pavlo's farm, this group of Nazis decided that they would stay at the farm.

It started with Brisko. He barked and barked, and it was his alarm bark.

We knew something was terribly wrong. Because of Brisko, *we knew*. So we went as far into the hay as possible and knew not to make any sounds. Brisko warned us, and they came. One black night they came with their horses, and we never knew light again until it was over.

I remember when they came. I heard Pavlo jogging alongside their horses across the field, and I risked a peek out of the barn slats. I saw their troop, and they had their horses with them. Brisko was circling them, ignored but barking and hollering. He knew what they were. The dog knew that they were coming for us. I cannot tell you how, but we all knew that the dog was there because he knew we were in danger. He was trying to protect us.

My first thought was of my boots and how it was already too late to lace them up. Pavlo was arguing with one of the Nazis.

"I promise," Pavlo told him, "it will be much more comfortable for them inside of the barn. Outside there are pests, and there is the weather to worry about."

"It's fine," said the German solider. "The horses are comfortable in the outside."

"The Nazis are going to stay here," my father whispered to me. "You mustn't make any noise at all, Libe!"

He put his hand over my mouth and kept it tight. My mother looked terrified, but my father stayed her panic with a new light from behind his eyes.

"I insist," said Pavlo to the Nazi soldier. "It would be my honor."

"Fine, old man!" replied the Nazi. "Just shut up already."

My father looked relieved, and my mother tilted her head as if to ask why.

Brisko's wild, desperate calls continued to echo unheeded about the farmland. The dog must have wondered why Pavlo was leading these murderers to their prey instead of fighting them off. Brisko's barks grew madder and shriller the closer the group came.

Brisko knew of the danger we were about to be in.

"Pavlo has convinced the Nazis to house their horses here, too," he whispered ever softer. "This way any noises the soldiers hear might be blamed on the horses. Still, we must be more careful than ever."

And that's how it was. The Nazis moved into our barn, and so did their horses. I had thought that we were as far buried, as far into the hay, as far away from the light of day, as far into death, and as far from the glory of life that we could get. I was wrong. We went further in, deeper and deeper, until we were suffocated.

The Nazis slept directly above us, on top of the hay in which we sat curled in silence like three unborn babies awaiting the next world. We were silent as death, but thank goodness that Pavlo had the foresight to convince the soldiers to stay with their horses. Those horses provided much-needed cover for us. Those horses also became like companions to us. Brisko had disappeared.

Every once in a while, I would brave a peek out of the barn slats, search the field for Brisko, but he never came around to us. I hadn't realized how much strength that dog had given me, just by providing us with a glimpse of his figure in the moonlight. Now that he had gone, probably kept tied up near the house by Pavlo so as not to disturb the Nazis, I felt more alone than ever. The horses helped, but they were no Brisko. Brisko had known us, had known our plight. He'd been there to save us. The horses were just there.

One dog and one little girl. One dog that I never touched. He must have been an angel.

Pavlo came daily and tended to the Nazis, brought them food and water, and tended to their horses. During that time, I don't know how he managed to sneak us food. I don't remember. I only remember sitting there in utter silence with my father's hand over my mouth, feeling very much like I had been buried alive again, longing to see Brisko, wishing to be a bird, to be a cat, to be anything but me. If only I was a flea on Brisko's back! What a glorious life that would be.

We heard the soldiers talking, laughing. Sometimes it got so quiet that we heard the inhale of a cigarette.

We lived, barely alive, but in constant fear. We couldn't sneeze; we couldn't cough. We went to the bathroom where we sat. There was no way to empty the pot anymore. It was a time that I wished I was dead. It was a time that I already felt dead. But I wasn't dead. I was alive.

And you know what? We didn't give ourselves up. And you know what else? We didn't kill ourselves. We kept hiding. We kept quiet. My father kept his hand tightly shut on my mouth. We kept eating scraps of bread and sitting with mice. We kept scratching our lice. We stayed alive. We kept surviving. Why did we do that? How did we do that? Well, let me tell you a little secret—and this is coming from someone who has been to the darkest of the dark places—no matter how awful it looks outside or inside, no matter how many of life's essentials disappear, no matter how terrible today is, there is always the *hope* that tomorrow will be better. This is why we kept on. And let me tell you one more little secret, it *did* get better.

Six weeks into the Nazis stay at our barn, I heard a sound I'd missed: Brisko. The dog was barking on the east side of the field, and as the dog got closer, I could hear that he was following a man on horse. When the man arrived at Pavlo's house, Pavlo directed him to the barn. It was a Nazi soldier. He came into the barn and we could not see him, but we heard him. He came in and reported to the other soldiers that the war was over and that they should leave. Liberation, the time of freedom, had finally come.

We Start by Crawling

I t took a day or two for the soldiers to leave, but we stayed in the barn for weeks afterward. We were still afraid. Pavlo said that his neighbors would kill all of us if they knew he had been harboring Jews during the war. The anti-Jewish sentiment lasted years after the war was over. In many places, it still exists.

In fact, there were many Jews just like us who had stayed hidden in horrible conditions throughout the duration of the war, and when they finally came out and returned to Tuchin, after having managed to survive the entire time, they were killed right away. This happened all over the place, not just in Tuchin. Jews were sought and killed for months after the war officially ended. This is why so many Jews decided to leave their homes after the war. Many went to the United States of America. Others wanted a place to call their own, a special country that would protect the Jews in case something as horrible as the Holocaust ever happened again. This idea, which was not a new one by any means, became the birth of Israel, the modern country.

But at the end of the war, we were not in the promise land; we were still in the barn. When Pavlo finally thought that it was safe enough for us to return to the town, we crawled out of the barn. Yes, we crawled. We couldn't walk, you understand. Even my father couldn't walk, though he had been able to walk on occasion with Pavlo. For over a year and a half we were scrunched and crouched, but the last six weeks of utter stillness had crippled us all. We literally crawled out of the barn with the aid of sticks for support. We were leaving the barn no stronger than a baby just born into the world. It was painful, and we didn't really even feel free yet. My parents and I were so used to hiding and being afraid that it took a long time to let go of that feeling.

We only had one thing on our minds at that point. You see, during the entire time we hid, there was one thing we talked about more than anything else.

"Thank goodness," my mother would say. "Thank goodness for Channah. At least we know she is safe and comfortable, and if we never get out of here alive, she will live on."

And my father would nod his bent head in agreement.

"And if we do get out of here alive," he would say, "we'll find her and take her back."

So when we left the barn, our first mission was to track down my sister. Pavlo prepared us to leave.

"Pavlo," my father said, "You saved our lives. G-d knows what you've done, and his reward for you will be greater than anything I can possibly say to you now."

We all hugged him. I never got to say good-bye to Brisko. In fact, I never touched that dog. He had brought me out of death, carried me, all without touching. I remember his bark today. I remember his figure standing up in the moonlight, I remember his brilliant soul.

Right before we left, Pavlo handed something to my father. It was the gold watch that we had given him before we went into hiding.

"No," my father said. "You keep this. It is the least we can do."

"Isaak," said Pavlo." I cannot take this watch. It is your wife's. What I did was not for gold. It was for love."

Soon after, we left Pavlo's farm, that brave farmer, Brisko, and the barn that seemed like some broken gateway to a lost world. I was never more glad to cross a river.

What Happened to Channah

We crawled into Tuchin. Crawled. I couldn't manage to walk, my father was stiff, and my mother was weak. We took turns supporting each other. We dug our hands and fingernails into the dirt to move us along. It would have been pitiful if it hadn't been so painful. It took us hours, and we were afraid of being killed the whole while. But we could only think of seeing our Channah again.

After getting into town, we explored and asked questions only to people we had known and trusted. We asked the Russian soldiers. We discovered that besides us, there were five Jews from Tuchin who survived. Five out of three thousand.

There was a place set up for the surviving Jews, just a small house. We shared our horrors with each other. We learned that about six weeks after my father had left Channah at our old house, there had been an announcement. The Nazis, furious about the debacle at the ghetto, declared that all Jews would be found and killed. They said that anyone caught harboring a Jew would be found out and killed. They said that they would go house-to-house.

The principal's wife grew afraid. She and her husband told Channah to go and find her father, sending her out to fend for herself. Channah was only eleven years old.

Channah obeyed and went into the streets, where she was caught by an old schoolmate of hers who recognized her and called the Germans. The soldiers punched and beat her and tried to find out where she was going. She knew where we were. If it had been me, I would have spilled everything; I would have told them. But not Channah. My sister never told the Nazis where we were. She was strong. So they tortured her until they killed her.

Until this day, I have a strange daydream. I'll be sitting on a bus or a train and I'll turn around. I'll see my sister, and I'll smile at her. And I'll say, "Thank you."

Epilogue: Why We Survive

Today my name is Laura and that is my story.

Some people would say that my story is *beshert,* guided by destiny. Many Holocaust survivors have a similar feeling about their survival stories, and everyone feels very lucky to be alive.

Some time after World War II, my family moved to the United States. Later, my father helped Pavlo reach the status of the Righteous Among the Nations, also known as Righteous Gentiles, non-Jews who risked their lives to save Jews during the Holocaust. The Yad Vashem museum in Israel pays tribute to these courageous individuals who stood by the Jews during a time of persecution and tragedy.

Righteous Gentiles lived in or near countries affected by the Holocaust. They were regular citizens, just as you are in your own country. They were normal people living normal lives. For some reason or another, a group of these people known to us now, decided to secretly go against the Nazis in order to save the lives of Jews. It is very important to understand that these people existed and that they saved many lives, including my own. This honor was also later given to Pavlo's children.

Two of Pavlo's daughters came to the United States many years later, and I showed them New York City and Florida, where my father lived before he passed away. Gala, one of his daughters, still lives on Pavlo's farm to this day. Pavlo's brother never knew we had been hidden on the farm.

Today I am a mother of three: two doctors, one pharmacist. I'm a grandmother of six. If neither I nor my parents had chosen not to persist, none of my beautiful family would exist today. My brother, who was born shortly after the war ended, is also a doctor.

I am so proud of my brother, who I practically raised. He lives in Texas today with his family and their dog, Brisko.

I am still surviving.

Appendix

Author's Note

Whenever there is a story with a responsibility behind it, as is the case with *Brisko: A True Tale of Holocaust Survival*, there should be clarification regarding the author's process and his sources.

My process began with a series of in-depth, face-to-face interviews with Laura, the narrator of *Brisko*, who goes by the name Libe in this story and during the time of the war. I studied a video of Laura telling her family's story, which she had recorded some years earlier, and I studied a video that Laura's father had recorded a few months before he died, in which he also told their story. I took all accounts and began my research.

I used the online resources of museums like Yad Vashem in Israel, where I discovered digitized photographs of Laura's family, Pavlo and his farm, and of course Brisko the dog. Through a multitude of online resources, I studied maps of Tuchin and the historical timelines of events in the Ukraine and surrounding areas during World War II. I researched firsthand and secondhand accounts of the Tuchin revolt from various reference books found at the Holocaust Resource Center at Stockton College in New Jersey. I studied these facts and timelines and then placed the events of Laura's story into larger pictures of the war.

Most of Laura's account fit perfectly into history. There were some aspects of her story that were out of sync with historical timelines. In these instances, I stuck with the historical timelines. In one other instance, where Laura's story diverged slightly from her father's, I chose to tell Laura's story as she remembered it. That incident involved the painful account of how Laura's sister, Channah, came to be in the principal's household. There is nothing in the book that contradicts anything I found in my research.

The characters of Getzel and his boys are also historical. I did thorough research on their recorded actions and their part in the Tuchin revolt.

There are some parts in the book where I, writing as Laura, imagine what certain characters might have said or done when Laura had no knowledge of these characters' words or actions. This was done sparingly, and only to help the reader along in the story. Any time this occurs, it is stated that Libe is "imagining" or "wondering" what these characters "might" be saying or doing.

I am not a historian, nor am I a student of Holocaust studies. I am foremost a storyteller, one who wishes to help Laura reach the world with this important historical account. Laura has become a dear friend of mine through this process. Laura and her story have helped shaped my life in ways that I could not have predicted when I started this book. I hope that it will do the same for children, young adults, and adults around the world for decades to come.

Yiddish Glossary

beshert. Guided by destiny

cholent. Slow-cooked brisket stew

Gestapo. Nazi secret police (German)

hutzpah. Boldness, nerviness

Jude. Jew

Judenrat. Jewish committees designed to carry out anti-Jewish policies

pogrom. Organized massacre of people

Shabbos. Jewish Sabbath

schnell. Hurry (German)

shtetl. Small Jewish town in eastern Europe in the past

Yom Kippur. An important Jewish holiday when Jews fast and atone for their sins of the past year

Common Core Standardized Review

Standard: CCSS.ELA-Literacy.RI.6.3

Analyze in detail how a key individual, event, or idea is introduced, illustrated, and elaborated on in a text (through examples or anecdotes).

CCSS.ELA-Literacy.RI.6.6

Determine an author's point of view or purpose in a text and explain how it is conveyed.

Section One

1. Who is telling the story? Why would the author want to tell this story from a "first person" perspective?

2. Most of the story is told in chronological order. Why is the beginning of the story NOT told like this?

3. Infer why Libe can't speak after her attack. Cite textual evidence from the story to support your answer.

4. The author states:

   "There were people on the street, and outside the noise of the planes was much louder. They roared through the sky like griffins. I could see that everyone was heading to the forest. I didn't understand what the sound of planes meant."

   What can you infer is happening? Cite textual evidence from the story to support your answer.

5. In the third chapter, "Red Ribbons," why does Libe want her ribbons removed?

6. On September 1, 1939, the Russians took over Poland. Describe how this event changes daily life for Libe and the other Polish citizens.

7. Define the word *shtetl*.

8. In 1941, which world power replaced Russia as Poland's ruler?

9. In "Here Come the Nazis," the author describes a horrific attack on Libe's family by the Nazis. Cite textual evidence to support the idea that this attack was an extremely dangerous situation.

10. In "The Bible Lifted," why does Libe's family think that she is dead?

11. In "The Bible Lifted," Libe's father replaces the "beautiful stained-glass windows" with "ugly wooden boards." Discuss the symbolism of that.

12. Who is the man who brings the eggs?

13. Why is Uncle Fridal killed?

14. Describe what we know about Libe's family by the end of section one. Cite evidence from the text to support your answer.

Section One Extension

A. Working in a group, discuss a time when you felt discriminated against for being "different." This could be discrimination based on your race, religion, heritage, physical appearance, etc. After your discussion, work with your group to create a skit of someone being discriminated against and what you could do as a bystander to help the victim.

B. The author mentions the stained-glass windows in Libe's house several times. Using art supplies, design what you think the windows would have looked like before they were destroyed. Add a picture or symbol in the middle of the window that conveys a theme or message from *Brisko*. Under the window, write a brief description of what this symbol has to do with section one of *Brisko*.

C. Pretend that you are Libe and write a diary entry about one of the events that takes place in section one. Describe the event and discuss how the situation makes you feel and the questions that you might have.

Section Two

1. Why is it important for Libe to still have a "sense of humor" (25)?

2. Looking at the first chapter in section two, "The Slaughterings," cite textual evidence to prove that Libe's injuries are very severe.

3. Libe talks about people not wanting to part with their possessions. Why would they care about these things during a time like this? Is there anything that you would not want to part with, no matter what the circumstances were?

4. At the end of "The Principal," the narrator says that her family's house was being taken "easy as pie, like taking candy from a baby." Why does the author describe taking the house like that?

5. Describe the job of the Judenrat.

6. Where is Pavlo's farm located?

7. Who does the SS officer "save" in the family at the end of "The Escape"?

8. Use context clues from the beginning of "The Lucky Colors" to define the terms "downtrodden" and "resigned."

9. The fifth chapter in section two, "The Ghetto and the Seeds of Fire," describes the ghetto that Libe and her family was forced to live in. Write a descriptive paragraph and use contextual evidence to describe the ghetto.

10. Why does Libe's father not leave with Pavlo and the rest of the family when they escape from the ghetto?

Section Two Extension (class activity)

A. Put the Judenrat on trial. Choose a side and either defend or prosecute the Judenrat.

Break your class up into two groups:
Defense
Prosecution

Have your class create a mock trail. Assign lawyers and witnesses to design a defense and prosecution for the Judenrat. Your class can get as elaborate as time allows. Invite other classes to act as an audition and jury to the trial once the assignment is complete!

B. Section two of the book takes place one year after the end of section one. Write your own chapter of the book describing what happens to Libe and her family during that year.

C. Libe mentions that the Jews in her town had no idea what the Nazis were doing elsewhere around the world. Research a country besides Poland that was affected by the Nazis in World War II and create a presentation to describe what you learned.

Sections Three and Four

1. On page 44, Libe's mother questions whether Pavlo can be trusted, simply because he is Ukrainian. On page 59, when the family is in hiding at Pavlo's house, Libe says:

> "I began to consider this man. Here was a man, a Ukraine, who was risking his life, his family, and his livelihood for us. Who were we to him? My father's family, that's all. We were practically strangers. Pavlo was a tall man. He looked like a plain ordinary farmer. He had a great big forehead, the kind that was perfect for thinking, a pointed nose, with eyes close to it, and hollowed, well-defined cheek bones. He looked like a serious man, but his warmth and quiet nature let us know that he wasn't stern. And his actions let us know he wasn't a man at all; he was an angel among men."

Much like her mother in the second section of the book, Libe is worried whether Pavlo can be trusted, simply because he is Ukrainian. By page 59, however, she has total trust in Pavlo. What changes does Libe go through to make her like or dislike people for who they really are, despite where they come from or their ethnicity?

2. Pavlo does not tell his brother that he is hiding Libe and her family. We read:

> "'You will stay here,' Pavlo told us. 'You must be ready to run at any sign of the soldiers. My brother has no idea that I am hiding you here. It is very dangerous for us. If I am caught hiding Jews, they will treat my family as Jews and we will all be killed. Hopefully, this commotion will pass quickly. I will be by soon with some food for you both. After that, it would be best if you could try to get some sleep'" (60).

Imagine that his brother finds out. Write a conversation between Pavlo and his brother, where Pavlo defends his idea to hide the family. Pretend the two are arguing heavily and imagine the types of things Pavlo would say to convince his brother that Libe and her family deserve somewhere to stay.

3. Not only is Pavlo a very brave man for risking so much, he is also selfless. Find two examples from the book that prove he does not want the family to pay him back in any way.

4. Libe refers to her sister Channah as "lucky" to be living with the Lomtskas. Do you think Channah is really lucky, or is she living under just as much fear as Libe and her parents?

5. How does Channah exhibit bravery?

6. The first chapter of the book is titled "Buried Alive." At what other points in the book might Libe feel like she is being buried alive?

7. How does Brisko bring Libe such comfort and joy? Why do you think Brisko is aware of how evil the Nazis are?

8. While Libe is in hiding, she says:

> "I hated being me while we lived in the haystack. I wished I was
> anything but a little Jewish girl. When I heard a bird chirp in the
> distance, I wanted to be a bird. When I heard Brisko bark, I wanted
> to be a dog. I wanted to be a non-Jew, anything, even a cat, so that
> I could just sit outside without being afraid that I was going to get
> killed. Such a simple thought, just the idea of sitting outside on a
> step somewhere without being afraid that I was going to get killed
> for being a Jew. It's a terrible feeling, not wanting to be who you
> are" (79).

Libe has been forced into hating herself because of other people's discrimination toward her religion. Should she hate herself? How do people like
Pavlo and animals like Brisko make Libe feel better about herself?

9. Imagine you are forced to identify certain things about yourself (such as
your religion by wearing a yellow star, etc.), and those things cause people
to discriminate against you. Where would you find comfort?

10. Libe comments that "Brisko was part German shepherd. Maybe it was
that he shared a history with the enemy" (84). Does Libe mention his ties
to German roots for any reason? Does her love for Brisko, despite him shar-
ing a history with the enemy, say anything about Libe's character?

Section Five

1. How long does Libe and her family live on the farm?
2. How does the author create tension in the first chapter of section five? Site examples from the book to support your answer.
3. Why would Libe's family stay hidden in the barn weeks after hearing that they were free?
4. Why did Pavlo not keep the gold watch?
5. Besides Libe and her family, out of 3,000 Jewish people living in Tuchin before the war, how many survived?
6. Why did Libe want to say "Thank you" to her sister?
7. What does *beshert* mean?
8. Who were the Righteous Among the Nations?
9. What happens to Channah?
10. What happens to Libe after the war?

Section Five Extension

A. Libe mentions that her family never gave up and that is why they survived. Resilience was needed for all survivors of the Holocaust. Research another Holocaust survivor and tell their story.
B. After the war, many Jews like Libe left their home and traveled to other countries to start a new life. Use the Internet and other resources to find out where the Jewish people went after the war. Include the amount of people who went to each country when reporting on your research.
C. Libe's story of survival is special and, unfortunately, rare. Many more Jews lost their lives in the Holocaust than survived. Take a virtual tour of the Holocaust Museum in Israel. Learn something new that was not necessarily part of Libe's story and report your findings back to the class.

Community Outreach Project

Now that you have read *Brisko*, reach out to your community to find a group or organization in need. Like Brisko helped Libe and her family, it is now your class's job to do something positive for your community.

Decide on a problem that your community faces and figure out how you can help.

Working with your teacher, come up with a plan and put that plan into action.

Once complete, send the author your tale!
(TheSlitheryD@gmail.com)

Photos

Pavlo and Brisko pose with their family on the farm. Two Russian soldiers are seen in the background.

Pavlo and his wife pose on the farm.

Pavlo and his daughter pose on the farm. Brisko is at Pavlo's feet.

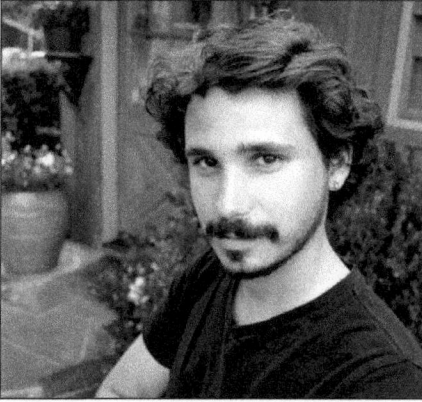

The Author

Steven Paul Winkelstein is an award-winning author of books for children. His *Elephant Alive!* series is adored by children all over the globe. Steven is known in the pirate-enthusiast community for his short story *The Squall*, published by 1018 Press. His book *Captain Kidd and the Jersey Devil* is due for release in summer 2015. He currently lives in Boulder, Colorado. He was born and raised in Margate City, New Jersey. You may email him at: TheSlitheryD@gmail.com

The Illustrator

Dana Juliano is an illustrator from Atlantic City, New Jersey. She majored in illustration at The University of the Arts in Philadelphia, Pennsylvania and graduated with a Bachelor's degree of Fine Arts. At The University of the Arts, Dana focused on the traditional side of illustration, mixing illustration and fine art. Dana currently resides in Oberlin, Ohio. Dana's work has been published twice in Temple University's Fourth Street Magazine.

CLEVERMORE

www.ingramcontent.com/pod-product-compliance
Lightning Source LLC
LaVergne TN
LVHW041224080426
835508LV00011B/1065